Tiger Tales

A Story of Survival

Written by Mary Peace Finley

TABLE OF CONTENTS

CelebrationPress
An Imprint of ScottForesman

In the Quiet of Night

Inga hasn't eaten all day. Now, deep inside her den at the Denver Zoo, she waits alone. No sounds disturb her. It's dark. Something is about to happen.

At eight o'clock the next morning, zookeeper Liz Hooton tiptoes to a tiny camera. She peeks into the den. Two cubs! By ten o'clock there are two more.

Inga has given birth to four healthy Siberian tigers—one of the most endangered animals on earth. And Liz can already tell that Inga's going to be a very good mother.

A Scary World Out There

For the first six weeks, Inga's babies stay in their den. When Liz opens the door, they flatten their ears. They hiss and huddle together.

Even though they're afraid, the cubs can't stay in the den forever. After six weeks, Dmitri, Serge, Sasha, and Helga creep into the Feline House exhibit. There are trees and rocks and cliffs and caves. Their new home is filled with scary sights, scary smells, scary shapes.

Over several days, one by one, the boards covering the exhibit windows are removed. Zoo visitors want to see the babies. But people get too close! Too noisy! Some people bang on the windows!

Inga charges at them and crashes into the glass. She grabs her cubs by their heads and legs and skin and drags them away. It's hard on the cubs, and it's hard on Inga. Zoo volunteers stand guard to keep people away from the windows.

In April, the cubs are almost five months old, and for the first time they go outdoors. They huddle on the concrete next to the building, mewing. Inga nudges them on. Cautiously, Dmitri steps out: Yipes! What's that? He races back. He's never been on dirt before and he's afraid of it.

Birds scare the cubs, too. So does wind. But every day they become more courageous. Every day, Inga leads them a little farther into their outdoor world.

The Moat

Dmitri spots the dry moat, a deep pit that separates the tigers from the people who have come to watch them. He creeps to the edge. Helga, then Serge and Sasha, follow him.

Inga jerks Helga back by the scruff of her neck. She cuffs Serge and Sasha. But there are four of them and just one of her. Finally, Inga tricks them all. She races behind them. The cubs' instinct to chase is so strong, they forget the moat and chase after her.

As the cubs grow, they all become more curious, but each one is different. Dmitri is brave. Helga is feisty. Sasha's a fraidy-cat. Serge is shy. They know better than to play near the moat, but they are too curious to stay away. It's fun to tug at the vines that trail down the sides. It's fun to bat at birds that flutter in the vines. It's fun . . . until oooOOOps! Dmitri falls straight to the bottom of the moat.

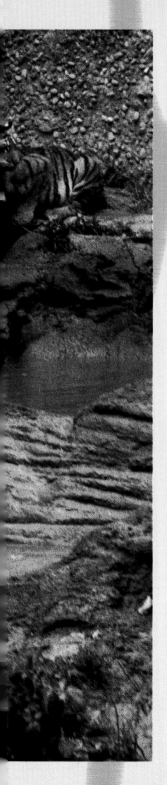

Dmitri isn't hurt when he lands. He bounces. He shakes his head, puzzled. Then he races back and forth at the bottom of the moat, looking up at his brother and sisters. Sasha, Serge, and Helga race back and forth along the edge, looking down at him.

Finally, Inga walks slowly to the moat. She chuffs at the top of a dark tunnel: *Come up this way!*

The tunnel is dark and scary, but Dmitri creeps in. When he comes out on top, his brother and sisters are still racing back and forth, looking down into the moat for him. Dmitri wonders what they are watching, so he runs to the edge and races back and forth, too. It takes them awhile to figure it out.

Tiger Training

When the cubs were helpless newborns, Inga protected them every minute. Now as they grow older, she begins to teach, train, and discipline them. The lessons are the same as in the wild—hunting and survival.

Inga swishes her tail for them to pounce on. She dashes through the tall grass. She lets them stalk her, jump on her, bite the back of her neck and legs and spine. Poor Inga! She's covered with lumps and scratches.

Like kittens playing, the cubs practice on each other, too.

One day Inga catches a magpie in the outdoor exhibit. She wounds it so it can't fly, then chuffs at Dmitri to come: *Stalk it! Catch it!* When he does, she takes it away and calls for another cub. Each one has a hunting lesson.

At eight months the cubs weigh almost a hundred pounds. But they still pile on Mom when they're afraid—four hundred pounds of them on one mom!

Today is July 18, the cubs' eight-month birthday. It's hot in Denver in the summertime, and Siberian tigers prefer cooler temperatures. Serge sprawls against Inga. He turns his head upside down and rubs it against his mother's cheek. He squirms. He stomps on Inga's stomach, then whacks his head into Inga's jaw so hard Inga's teeth snap together.

Slowly, without any anger, Inga rises. Then she sits on Serge and squashes him. Serge's paws stick out on all sides. He moans, but it's all part of tiger training!

Survival

As growing males, Dmitri and Serge play rougher than Helga and Sasha. Their paws are bigger. Their faces are fuller and less fuzzy. Soon their play fights will become real fights over food and space.

Adult tigers like to live alone. In the wild, male cubs leave home when they are about a year-and-a-half old. Females leave when they're two. But if these cubs had been born in the wild, chances are they would not have survived to become adults.

Siberian tigers are the biggest tigers in the world and are among the most endangered of all animal species. People are their only enemy. They are hunted for their hides and teeth and body parts. People cut down their forest homes. There is no safe place left in the natural world for Siberian tigers to live.

Will Inga's cubs be among the last Siberian tigers on earth? They may be, but the Denver Zoo and other zoos are working with a Species Survival Plan to keep endangered animals alive.

A total of six hundred Siberian tigers are still alive. Five hundred live in zoos and animal reserves. Only one hundred are left in the wild.

Helga, Serge, Sasha, and Dmitri will never live free in the wild. But with the help of zoos, new generations of tigers will be born in safety.